Zebras

Ashland Public Library
66 Front Street
Ashland, MA 01721

Leo Statts

abdopublishing.com

Published by Abdo Zoom™, PO Box 398166, Minneapolis, Minnesota 55439. Copyright © 2017 by Abdo Consulting Group, Inc. International copyrights reserved in all countries. No part of this book may be reproduced in any form without written permission from the publisher. Abdo Zoom™ is a trademark and logo of Abdo Consulting Group, Inc.

Printed in the United States of America, North Mankato, Minnesota
062016
092016

THIS BOOK CONTAINS RECYCLED MATERIALS

Cover Photo: Photocreo Michal Bednarek/Shutterstock Images
Interior Photos: iStockphoto, 1, 6–7, 10–11; Angelika Stern/iStockphoto, 4, 16; William Davies/iStockphoto, 5; Goddard Photography/iStockphoto, 7; Joel Shawn/Shutterstock Images, 8; W. L. Davies/iStockphoto, 9; Lucyna Koch/iStockphoto, 12–13; Red Line Editorial, 13, 20 (left), 20 (right), 21 (left), 21 (right); Shutterstock Images, 14; Lumen Digital/Shutterstock Images, 15; Peter Malsbury/iStockphoto, 17; Jamen Percy/iStockphoto, 18; Chantal de Bruijne/Shutterstock Images, 19

Editor: Emily Temple
Series Designer: Madeline Berger
Art Direction: Dorothy Toth

Publisher's Cataloging-in-Publication Data
Names: Statts, Leo, author.
Title: Zebras / by Leo Statts.
Description: Minneapolis, MN : Abdo Zoom, [2017] | Series: Savanna animals |
    Includes bibliographical references and index.
Identifiers: LCCN 2016941156 | ISBN 9781680792041 (lib. bdg.) |
    ISBN 9781680793727 (ebook) | ISBN 9781680794618 (Read-to-me ebook)
Subjects: LCSH: Zebras--Juvenile literature.
Classification: DDC 599.665--dc23
LC record available at http://lccn.loc.gov/2016941156

Table of Contents

Zebras 4

Body 8

Habitat 12

Food 14

Life Cycle 16

Quick Stats. 20

Glossary 22

Booklinks 23

Index 24

Zebras

Zebras are known for their stripes.

The stripes help them blend together. This keeps them safe from **predators**.

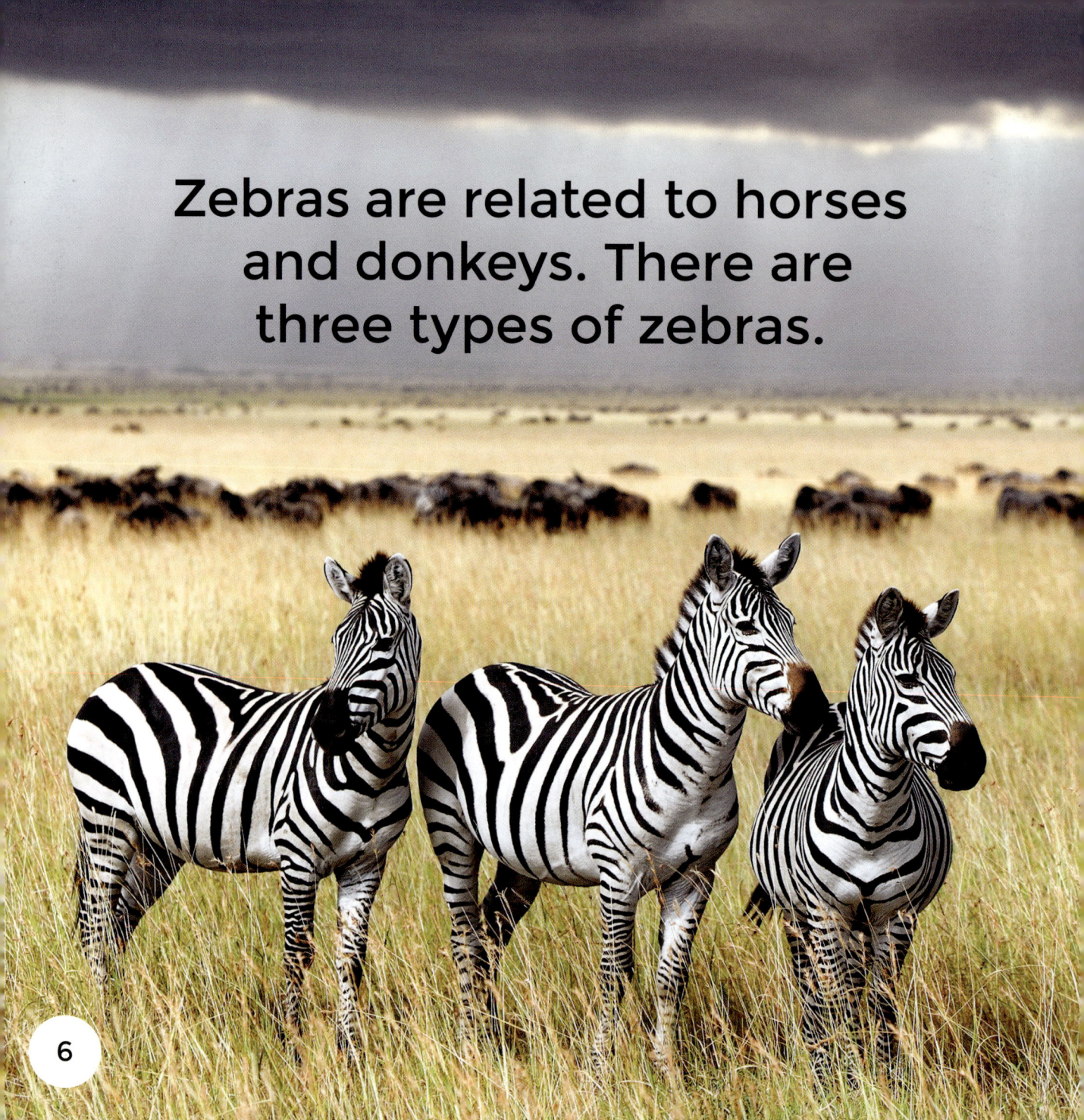
Zebras are related to horses and donkeys. There are three types of zebras.

The plains zebra
is the most common.

Body

Zebras have thick **manes**.
They also have stripes.

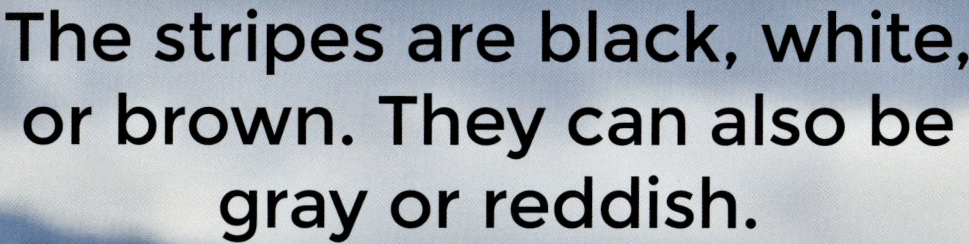

The stripes are black, white, or brown. They can also be gray or reddish.

The stripes confuse predators. They make it hard to see just one zebra.

This gives zebras more time to run away.

Habitat

Zebras live in Africa.
Some live in **savannas**.
Others live in the desert.

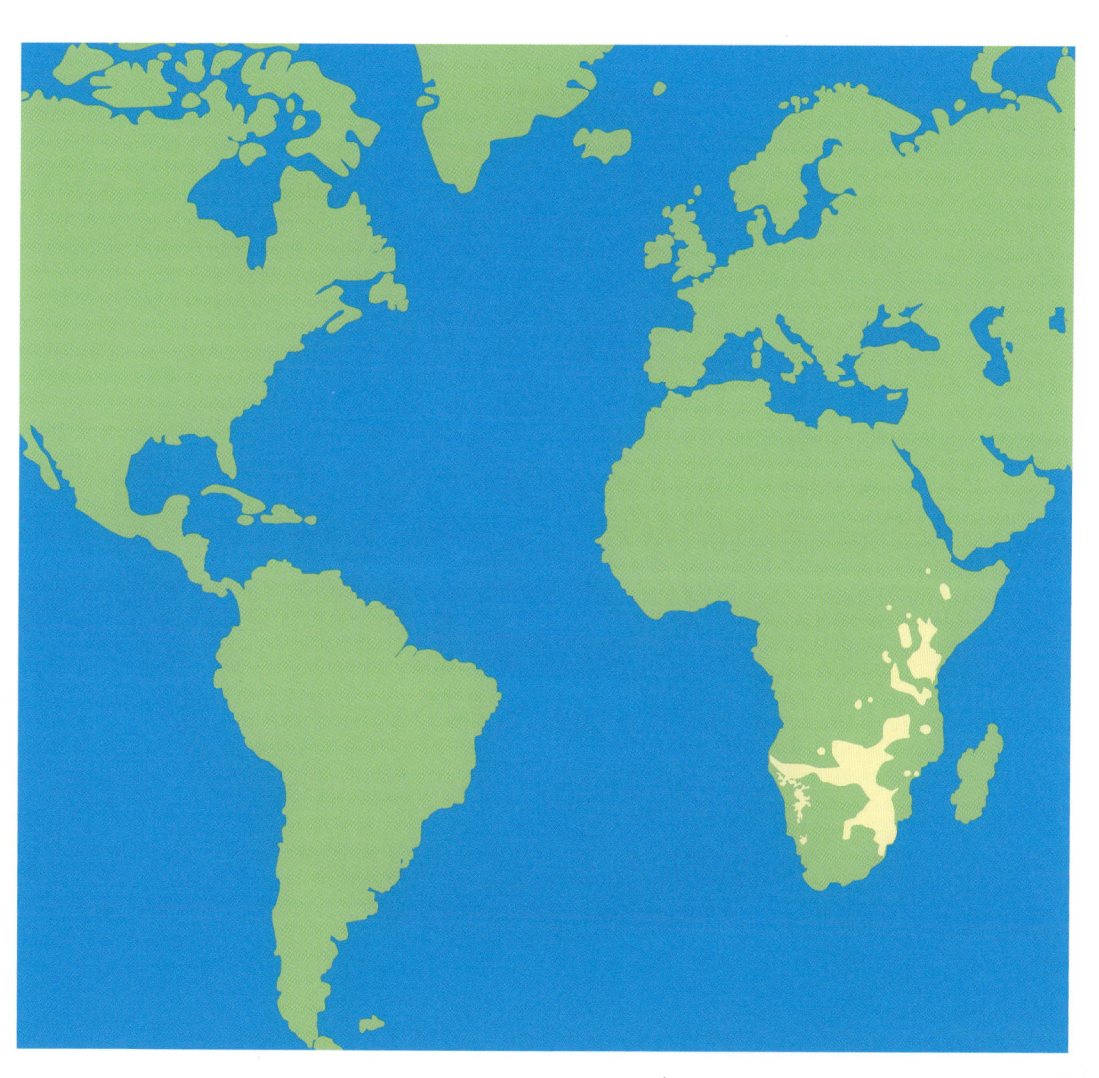

☐ Where zebras live

Food

Zebras eat plants.
They also need water.

Water is hard to find in dry seasons.
Zebras have to **migrate**.
They travel to lakes and rivers.

Life Cycle

Baby zebras are called **foals**.

After three years
they leave their mothers.

Zebras live in a **herd**.
A male zebra guards the herd.

Zebras live about 25 years.

Average Height

A zebra is shorter than a door.

5 ft

6 ft 8 in

Quick Stats

Average Weight

A zebra is heavier than a baby grand piano.

700 lbs   540 lbs

Glossary

foal - a baby animal.

herd - a group of animals.

mane - the longer hair that grows on an animal's neck and back.

migrate - to move from one place to another, often to find food or water.

predator - an animal that hunts others.

savanna - a grassland with few or no trees.

Booklinks

For more information on **zebras**, please visit booklinks.abdopublishing.com

Zoom In on Animals!

Learn even more with the Abdo Zoom Animals database. Check out **abdozoom.com** for more information.

Index

baby, 16

eat, 14

herd, 18

live, 12, 13, 18, 19

mane, 8

predators, 5, 10

stripes, 4, 5, 8

types, 6

water, 14, 15